SONNET STATION

A. Gee

Unsolicited Press
Portland, Oregon
www.unsolicitedpress.com
info@unsolicitedpress.com
619-354-8005

SONNET STATION
Copyright © 2026 A. Gee
All Rights Reserved.
Printed in the United States of America.
First Edition.
ISBN: 978-1-963115-76-5

No part of this book may be used or reproduced in any manner whatsoever without written permission except in the case of brief quotations embodied in critical articles or reviews.

This is a book of poetry. The people, places, and events described herein are either entirely fictional, grossly exaggerated, or so bizarrely true that you'd never believe me anyway. Any resemblance to actual persons (living, dead, or undead) is coincidental—unless they recognize themselves, in which case… yikes. All rights reserved, even the ones you didn't know existed.

Distributed by Asterism Books
https://asterismbooks.com/

For wholesale orders:
Asterism Books
568 1st Avenue South, Ste 120
Seattle, WA 98104
(206) 485-4829
info@asterismbooks.com

Cover Design: Kathryn Gerhardt
Editor: Summer Stewart

TABLE OF CONTENTS

The Crowns
    Sunday in the Park With Will   3
    In the Beginning   7
    Letters to the Editor   11

The Pushkins
    Search for Meaning   17
    The Age of Death   18
    Slavic Gods   19
    Dinner On St. Mark's Square   20
    Strict in Form and Measure   21
    Pursuit of Knowledge   22
    The Last Two Years   23

Juxtapositions
    Ozy Meets Harriet   27
    Dashboard Light   28
    Timely Sonnet   29
    Heirs to Tomorrow   30
    One True God   31
    Noir   32
    For Cyrano   33
    Grains of Sand   34

The Big Bang	35
And I Quote	36

Old School
Pictures at an Exhibition	39
Pencil Sketch	40
Footprints in the Sand	41
Moonset	42
Love Sonnets	43
Night and Day	44
To My Father	45

Places, Everybody
On Bourbon Street	49
Dear Florence	50
Jerusalem	51
Bryce	52
Ocean Views	53
Less Traveled	54
Easter Island	55
Always Have Paris	56
Sonnet Station	57

Commentary
Freedom's Price	61
Existential Questions	62
Tyrant	63

Banality of Evil	64
Metropolis	65

Seasonal
The Argument	69
Spring Serenade	70
Sails of Summer	71
Witch's House	72
Autumn	73
Yule	74

A Few Final Notes
Paganini	77
Csárdás Monti	78
Moonlight Sonata	79

Shall I count the ways? The patient reader will find I do in this book (and the impatient one can peek at page 36)

42. That was Douglas Adams' famous answer to everything. It's forty-three and counting for us as you open this book.
Forty-three incredible years. Looking at our grandkids' pictures, how lucky were we?

How lucky am I?

And finally, not one of those husbands to whom you can say, "You've never written me a poem."

Love,

Always.

The Crowns

SUNDAY IN THE PARK WITH WILL

"Prince Hamlet, got a minute for the press?"
He pauses, as if ready to reflect.
Diplomacy, adroitness, finesse
might work for some—I tend to be direct:
"Ophelia, by now I'm sure you've heard.
Do you accept responsibility?"
I find direct works best. The prince, now stirred,
inflates his chest—he's all nobility—
goes on, first about Yorik, life and death—
I interrupt: "It's you who drove her mad."
His monologues, he hardly takes a breath.
As to the lady, sure, it makes me sad.
The audience, though, has a need to know.
They've paid good money; we put up a show.

They've paid good money; we put up a show.
"Hey, Hecuba, go easy on that wine!"
A play within a play, a tale of woe.
Who's she to me? A lover, and quite fine.
Poor Yorik—turns out, not a speaking part—
but Hamlet's opportunities to ham
and speak his truth to reason and to heart
and to Horatio—to smash, to slam . . .
Ah, universal truth, how sweet you are.

Proclaimed up on the stage with such panache.
The dream of every actor —future star:
ask existential questions, for good cash!
I checked the playbill proofs; I get top billing.
Director interrupts: "Once more, with feeling!"

Director interrupts: "Once more, with feeling!"
It's kind of hopeless with his protégé
Behind the scenes, extensive wheeling-dealing,
and there he is, forgetting what to say,
and how to say it, "be or not to be,"
yet surely getting some outrageous sum.
I'd take the slings and arrows were it me.
For now, though, he's the one who's on the come.
I should have gone to law school like Mom said.
What does one do with a degree in drama?
I'd have two point three kids, a dog, be wed . . .
You hear me, kids? Do listen to your mama.
But you can't help it, can you? It's innate.
The staggering desire to be great.

The staggering desire to be great,
Ophelia a victim of its whims.
She dies, not by a cruel twist of fate,
nor by a killer's sword. Instead, it seems,
neglect and sheer abandonment's at fault.
A prince's will—as fickle as his mood,

and if mere words can constitute assault,
then surely of this most misunderstood
of princes . . . Hamlet seeks to reassure
that she was his true love and not forgotten.
How beautiful she was, how virgin, pure.
It isn't her, it's Denmark that is rotten.
Would Hamlet have been great, had he been king?
Some words are venom, but the play's the thing.

Some words are venom, but the play's the thing.
The audience must suffer with the artist,
and whether it is roses that they fling . . .
best wish that it's the kindest, not the smartest,
among them that drive sentiment online,
and trolls will troll the critics, not the playwright,
and pepper him with "wondrous" and "divine,"
and hope that someone's just as kind when *they* write.
It's funny how each part is called an "Act."
Alluding just to what, you surely guess.
Too intimate, or worse yet, too abstract,
accused of indecision or excess . . .
Find Goldilocks and put her in a cage.
A gilded one, and then the world's your stage.

A gilded one, and then the world's your stage.
Full of cliches, he was, and full of wisdom.
Used them all up. Now, how does one engage

the readers to amuse or to appease them
without encroaching on what's clearly Will?
I haven't given up on sounding clever,
nor will I in the future do so—still,
henceforward, I'll wholeheartedly endeavor
to keep my themes on dry and solid ground,
and chastise errant metaphors and grammar,
and stay away from Will: he's not around,
and sculpt using a chisel, not a hammer . . .
But I will miss the rose, by any name.
What's one more error? You know who to blame.

What's one more error? You know who to blame.
Most existential questions lack an answer.
The outer play resolves into the frame,
and Hecuba runs off with some young dancer.
Here is my chance: must catch him unawares.
His sweeping monologues will overpower.
The audience wants more: they must get theirs
(and later, we'll talk princes in the tower).
For now, though, Danish royalty's in town.
And I must get a statement on the record.
If heavy is the head that wears the crown,
then surely, it's because that record's checkered.
Well, I'm not here to judge, but I digress.
"Prince Hamlet, got a minute for the press?"

IN THE BEGINNING

In the beginning, God was growing tired
of everything and nothing, all at once.
Omnipotent, he nonetheless desired
to hear more than an echo in response
to a profound pronouncement on existence
or lack thereof—no matter how precise
or imprecise his language, in this instance,
and certainly not asking for advice,
God ultimately chose a course of action
that leads us, reader, to the present day.
The universe, no longer an abstraction,
and physics, not philosophy, holds sway,
though priests will still remind us from the dais:
It all began when God first ended chaos.

It all began when God first ended chaos.
He banished it, in truth, to nether regions.
The hosts maintained the order in their legions,
Beelzebub and Satan, Asmodeus,
have not yet fallen—time yet, to betray us.
No doomsday cults and no occult religions.
No doves, known as the holiest of pigeons,
Not even death, not born yet to decay us.
No—none of these were there, but there was light.

God thought about it and, because he could,
created evening followed by a night,
and then announced the combination good,
and it was evening, it was morning, bright.
Creation underway, the angels brood.

Creation underway, the angels brood,
as God makes land to stand on, and some plants,
and Satan feeling, well, misunderstood,
or having grown too tired of the chants,
required as they were within the hosts,
expresses discontent -- he's rather public—
and overheard by some in pithy boasts,
but Heaven, as you know, not a republic . . .
Should God have intervened right then and there?
The universe might take a different path.
But as it were, he didn't seem to care.
No signs as yet of Heaven's holy wrath.
Another night and day now stand complete,
as Satan thinks of voting with his feet.

As Satan thinks of voting with his feet,
God hangs the sun and moon up in the sky.
No outward sign of having gone awry,
our genesis, though still far from complete,
keeps rolling to its newly minted beat,
still lacking, though, in things that multiply.

The angels sing hosannas way up high,
but there is not as yet a beast to bleat
in harmony with them. The wind does wail.
The rain sates dusty plains, the oceans roar,
but there are none to hear the gusty gale,
or, having heard a song, to ask for more.
Cacophony of sound to no avail.
No listener to listen or adore.

No listener to listen or adore.
The thought occurs to God. It comes unbidden.
He's satisfied with what had come before.
Could he have done it faster? Well, he didn't,
but now decides to conjure up some whales
and shellfish too, and other bottom feeders,
and fish of every kind shine in their scales,
and flocks of every feather follow leaders.
Did birds believe they're angels on the wind?
Did krakens think the deep their sole dominion?
Who knows what it was like before man sinned?
Philosophers may render an opinion,
but even now, who knows the minds of raptors?
The Genesis was sparse in early chapters.

The Genesis was sparse in early chapters.
Time for the tale to render us some meat.
Put on the earth on Friday, with their captors,

the hairy beasts that suckle from the teat,
along with every kind of creepy crawly,
and chief among them, Satan as a snake.
Ostensibly still virtuous and holy,
but you and I both know what is at stake.
Did God do it on purpose, choosing Satan?
What other option is there, God is good.
He wanted us to fall, but then to straighten.
Be good, but only once we've understood.
As for the snake, it surely knows its part.
A phallic symbol for a hungry heart.

A phallic symbol for a hungry heart.
Eve, at this point, does not yet know of Adam.
Well, biblically, that is—she stares right at him—
no fig leaf to obscure his better part—
those haven't been invented, prior art—
she sees it not—the fact is, she can't fathom,
this ancient lady—can I call her madam—
just what is Adam's purpose, at the start?
Come Satan to the rescue—finds his calling—
and teaches Eve the meaning of the tree.
How sinuous his motion, how inspired,
If crawl you must, you best be good at crawling,
and Eve, having been taught, thinks that she's free.
And God declared the Sabbath and retired.

LETTERS TO THE EDITOR

Dear Editor: do you solicit sonnets?
If not, could I still send a few your way?
They're on a single theme and dwell upon its
exhaustive possibilities to sway
the reader or the editor, what have you
to my iambic, undisputed prowess.
Had the creator chosen to endow us—
yes, each and every one, with this same skill,
it wouldn't be remarkable, my quill,
and having found, within, nothing of value,
you surely would dispose of it as trash,
considering it nothing if not sassy,
and next time, just to read me, ask for cash.
(Enclosed, per your request, please find a S.A.S.E.)

Enclosed, per your request, please find a S.A.S.E..
Had you a chance to read these, may I ask?
They're good, right? Some are funny, some are classy,
but surely all are equal to the task.
Oh, btw, I did submit these elsewhere—
I swear I'll let you know if any print—
but waiting to hear back is such a nightmare.
(Prefer your publication, though, hint, hint).
I now go by a newly minted byline,

or if you would prefer, a nom de plume.
My day job, high above Manhattan's skyline . . .
If they found out, they'd laugh at me on Zoom.
Well, time to go—can't wait for your response.
It's time for a poetic renaissance!

It's time for a poetic renaissance!
Eschew these new, at best unproven forms!
Let's write just as the giants did, for once.
The anguish and despair of college dorms,
assembled so by rambling laureates
into a hash of adjectives and feeling,
(with the assistance of euphoriants)
enough to send but any mind to reeling . . .
Where's the appreciation for the art?
The rhyme is banished, sent to autre lieu.
Thus, in my every sonnet, Bonaparte
is forced to fight, once more, his Waterloo.
So just a quick reminder—read it yet?
Not my intent to pester—don't forget!

Not my intent to pester—don't forget
that recently you've gained a new subscriber,
and by reminding, I don't mean to bribe, or . . .
but anyway, attached, find a vignette.
I think it might just be the best one yet.
My soul is in it, wholly, every fiber.

It mentions Florence, Rome, so too the Tiber,
in writing it, I worked up quite a sweat.
Could you, perhaps, provide another pointer?
That last critique was helpful, but of course,
one cannot help but feel that the rejoinder
referring to a jackass and a horse
was at yours truly. Still, I'll reconnoiter . . .
Try, find another outlet, can't do worse.

Try, find another outlet, can't do worse.
Much easier to say than is to do,
for these are times that one might call adverse
to roses, be they red or be they blue.
Why can't they have them blue, at any rate?
Those scientists, armed as they are with CRISPR.
The poet's flower need no longer wait,
and lovers with blue roses need not whisper.
The world it seems, has room for every kind
except for scribes that wish to ply their verses.
Those will be met with kicks in the behind.
What's worse—complete oblivion, or curses?
My roses shall be blue from this day forward.
The book is almost finished, writing foreword.

"The book is almost finished, writing foreword . . ."
Oh, that's great news, Dear Poet, carry on!
Where do we go, as poets, if not forward?

The breath of your submissions! Pantheon
of heroes and protagonists—impressive!
Vocabulary pure, pristine, expressive!
But sadly, for these poems, not for us.
Please do not query further, or harass
the staff: they simply look for other forms.
You surely understand art is subjective.
As poetry evolves, so do its norms,
and as you write, you must retain perspective . . .
Remember, different strokes for different folks.
Restraining order? My assistant jokes!

"Restraining order? My assistant jokes!"
That was the last I heard of that submission.
I cancelled my subscription—what a hoax.
Now this, my new, most precious composition,
is looking for a reputable home.
As I search far and wide for metric rhyme,
and stumble on your outlet as I roam . . .
I hope you'd take a look—it's been a climb,
but sure feels like the road that led to heaven.
Kept notes along the way, a type of journal.
Now at the top—well, technically there's seven—
as in the hills on which Rome stands, eternal,
each tied into a bow, as cute as bonnets.
Dear Editor: Do you solicit sonnets?

The Pushkins

SEARCH FOR MEANING

Most recently, I've searched for meaning,
and I'll admit it: I'm a slouch.
Imagine, though, my weekly cleaning,
and I find meaning in the couch!
Next to a few forgotten quarters,
receipts from ancient take-out orders,
a candy wrapper, I think Mars,
and free-drink coupons from some bars.
Well, that's accomplished; what's for dinner?
I'm full of purpose and resolve,
doubts melt, evaporate, dissolve,
and can it be? I'm feeling thinner.
Just a quick search, that's all it took.
Now off to write my self-help book.

THE AGE OF DEATH

The age of death arrived—it's stealthy—
and suddenly I'm losing friends.
Some were just getting by, some wealthy;
their means don't justify their ends.
Some go away unseen, discreetly—
I find them written up, so sweetly
on social media, with love.
Some struck by lightning from above.
I fear it, though the fear's receding
and resignation's setting in;
obsessing about "might have been,"
debating with myself, succeeding,
deciding that I matter still
and so go on, by force of will.

SLAVIC GODS

Perun', the Thunder God, jails Veles,
and peace and justice rule the land,
but the shape shifter, ever jealous,
escapes forthwith as he had planned.
The world descends to war and chaos.
The priests preach vengeance from their dais',
and shamans call for sacrifice;
fruit offerings shall not suffice.
As tribe by tribe men join the battle,
the gods rest, watching from above,
death is a symbol of their love;
the slain, their sacrificial cattle.
To Slavic gods, like all the rest,
two warring brothers taste the best.

DINNER ON ST. MARK'S SQUARE

St. Mark's Square, pianos playing,
pigeons flutter under foot.
"Two for dinner?" hostess saying.
Winds chime in, I hear a flute.
The clock's zodiac is striking,
the concerto's to its liking.
Pisces shows on the big dial;
we might be here for a while.
Here they come, the lords and ladies.
Masquerade is in full force,
though the waitress had seen worse;
daemon coming straight from Hades
laughing at us, swipes our wine.
They'll bring more; we're here to dine.

STRICT IN FORM AND MEASURE

"Make sure your poem has a meter,"
the teacher said in English class,
and claimed: if it is to be literature,
it must be written thus.
A poem's not a game of inches;
it stretches, shrinks, offends, and pinches,
though it is easier to perform
if it conforms to proper norm.
The good news? I don't need a ruler.
My telephone can measure length,
requiring no skill or strength.
So let him call out, Bueller, Bueller.
He'll get a poem, one of mine,
and ending on the fourteenth line.

PURSUIT OF KNOWLEDGE

Ah, Ozymandias, in college;
I think it was in English class,
still in pursuit of carnal knowledge,
struck up a convo with a lass.
I wasn't sure about my chances;
my weak attempts—you'd say advances,
did not at first amount to much.
But lyrics, rock, she liked as such.
I first impressed her with Tom Sawyer,
Rush, gilded cage, a Shakespeare riff,
and my performance, a bit stiff,
at least did not seem to annoy her,
and though I laid it on too thick,
Ozy and Ozzy did the trick

THE LAST TWO YEARS

Another call. The faces take their places.
A choreographed dance, fit for the stage.
Cliched, exhausted, hackneyed social graces
and tedious routines refuse to age:
"Oh, hahaha, I think you are on mute,"
"I'm loving your new background, it's so cute!"
A few more fits and starts, the meeting lingers.
I push it to the side, my nimble fingers
are working on a Wordle while they chat.
I cannot mute it though, might miss a question
and get invited to another session.
(Yeah, fitting words to boxes is all that!)
The last two years, you ask? They have been trying.
But all in all, preferable to dying.

Juxtapositions

OZY MEETS HARRIET

I met a traveler from a modern land,
and she's like: "Don't you give me any lip!
Lie *here*—stay partly covered by the sand.
This picture will remind me of my trip."
The stylish shades obscure her upper face,
but few would doubt the strength behind that tone,
known as it is to kings through time and space,
and so I pose with her, a silent stone.

Thus captured, she will send me through the air:
"His name was Ozymandias, King of Kings"
and others will reply: "Wish I was there!"
and add "Oh, L.O.L, what ARE those things?"
And I'll stay here, refusing to decay.
The sand dunes that preserve stretch far away.

DASHBOARD LIGHT

A sonnet should be scandalous, why not?
What should I call you, love, if not my peach?
Veiled, hidden innuendos, guarded speech . . .
Remember how we'd nearly gotten caught,
the Henny, Swiss fudge cookies that you'd brought,
my ancient clunker parked right by the beach . . .
That silly day seems safely out of reach,
and yet my mouth still waters at the thought . . .

How precious was your each and every touch?
The endless wait between those seaside trips . . .
Our hands in search of anything to clutch.
Your shallow breath and crimson, pouty lips.
Did we find paradise? Well, not as such,
but enter it we did, between your hips.

TIMELY SONNET

"The future is as present as the past,"
the physicist exclaimed, a beer in hand.
"The paradoxes, since you haven't asked,
resolve themselves. I wish you'd understand!"
He said this, then he took another sip,
and looked at me as if I was from Mars.
Confusing, but I need to get a grip;
looks like I found the guy, so many bars . . .
I play along and hiccup —"there's no time???
It's really an illusion, all for show?"
"Go back," he said, "kill grandpa, that's a crime.
But he won't be your grandpa, that I know."
That sealed it, so I shot him on the spot.
Turns out he's right, and Grandma was a slut.

HEIRS TO TOMORROW

What is our need to matter? Will machines,
when they achieve a sentient state at last,
will they have pride? Or is it in our genes,
a relic of some atavistic past?

My Roomba's yet to try to take me out—
concern about its inner works persists.
Just what will happen when it starts to doubt;
to ponder whether it, in fact, exists?

The laptop's safely anchored to the wall,
so likely can't effectuate a coup.
The Roomba, though, it well knows how to roll,
as to the stairs—so far it has no clue.

Are AI vacuums our predestined heirs?
Who knows, but to be safe, I sleep upstairs.

ONE TRUE GOD

Emerging from the shadow of the moon,
the Aten takes his place among the gods.
Young Tutankhaten makes as if to swoon—
drops to his knees in thanks. His father's squads

are jealous in the guarding of their law,
but secretly, the prince does not believe.
How could this be the god of gods? He saw
that Khonsu did eclipse him as the eve

wore on. Are any of them gods? Or not?
More likely, they're the workings of a clock.
The prince knows it is heresy. The thought
persists, however, as his father's flock

beats heads down on the granite, grateful for
the Aten: May he rule forever more.

NOIR

She walked across the room, a feral cat,
a gait to make a man weak at the knees.
Her bodycon sheer black, and she, all that,
took out a cigarette, and gestured: please.

I fumbled for a lighter, hands unsteady.
No luck—pants pocket jingling with loose change.
The desk's top drawer came to the rescue. Ready,
she bent her face towards me. "Something strange,"

she said, a kitten toying with a mouse,
"is happening. My husband's not been home.
Can you find out if he's a cheat? the louse.
Please bring him back, wherever he may roam."

Recovering, I nod, light a cigar.
I should have known it will be a noir.

FOR CYRANO

I once had the misfortune to attack
(for as they say, in ignorance, there's bliss)
none other than Messier de Bergerac,
and all over a trifle—just a kiss.

Oh, had I known the gentleman's sharp tongue,
I surely would have been more circumspect;
but as it was, equating me to dung
was merely the beginning, I expect.

What does one do, when abject ridicule
gets punished with an equitable turn?
When seeking to paint someone else a fool
gets paid back, and in kind? When will I learn?

Full of contrition, I shall thus compose
the story of one beaten by a nose.

GRAINS OF SAND

As memories flood in, the clock stands still.
The second hand is helpless. The deluge
sweeps all that's in its path. The evening's chill
seeps into every bone, there's no refuge.
His wife, that first shy smile, and then a laugh!
"A boy! Yes, it's a boy! I'm calling Mom!"
The hospital, so helpful, and its staff
so sensitive . . . No matter, he is numb.
Was it all worth it, ups and downs of note?
His children here, their children matter most . . .
"Say something . . ." But the words die in his throat.
A sob escapes, the wailing of a ghost.
He is no longer here. His form remains.
The hourglass relents. Sand falls in grains.

THE BIG BANG

If there's a rhyme or reason to the world,
a purpose that is yet to be revealed,
I'm losing hope of seeing it unfurled.
Opaque as ever, it remains concealed.

I do not speak of insight or of truth.
Eurekas that light up with sudden flare
were surely present, more so in my youth.
Indeed, I've had enough of them to spare.

But genuine profundity escapes,
and wisdom doesn't lag too far behind.
And purpose? Not a hint of how it shapes
the universe. A challenge to our kind.

Perhaps it's really just "let there be light,"
to puzzle us, bewilder, and delight.

AND I QUOTE

Quite recently, I've found a new technique
for complimenting my disgruntled lover.
No need for mystery, nor for mystique.
It is the Bard himself that gives me cover.
You see, I've found he has one fifty-four.
One fifty-four! And each a better sonnet
than I could ever write, so I adore
and serenade her with them. How? I'm on it:
I wouldn't dare to borrow from the Bard.
His ghost would haunt me and disturb my slumber.
The answer, and it's really not that hard.
She says: Say something nice. I pick a number.

Old School

PICTURES AT AN EXHIBITION

A still shot, water droplets stopped, midair;
sun, incandescent, rainbow on their skins,
and I, when I first see those eyes, and stare,
stop breathing: life ironically begins
when you are yanked from merely being on.
Confronted with an existential pulse:
Her! No one else! No masterpiece yet drawn
can rival her. My want, a flock of gulls.
I hunger, noisy, caution to the wind.
She's looking back—oh, what a precious crumb!
My dreams are not yet dashed, but they are pinned
on hope, irrational, that she'd succumb.
What miracle life is, how sweet its bite,
to give us lust, and lovers at first sight.

PENCIL SKETCH

Could I but draw, I'd sketch you day and night.
I'd capture your sweet cheek line as a peach,
the soaring eyebrows as a bird in flight,
the lips a gentle wave upon the beach.

I'd draw your eyes as rainbows through the dark,
your hair as raven feathers, deepest black.
Your smile as lightning, blinding with a spark.
A graceful swan will model for your back.

I'd draw no landscapes and no nature morte,
no flower vases and no setting sun;
no vain cartoons one draws for fun or sport.
I have no need of subjects: I have one.

I cannot draw, but you're on every page.
Still beautiful. Still mine. Still young. I age.

FOOTPRINTS IN THE SAND

Our love, like gentle footprints in the sand
first softened, and then overrun by waves,
now barely visible in outline, flat and bland.
A hint of what once was, these shallow graves.

Like carefree flotsam tossed into the spray,
we traveled with the current, duty-free,
mistaking our proximity for play,
and all the while abandoned to the sea.

What happened to us? Was it just the years
exerting their inexorable pull
as grain by grain, replaced by salty tears,
made every touch mundane, and passions cool?

Here, take my hand. Let's walk this sandy beach.
The tide is low. The waves are out of reach.

MOONSET

Come, love, and let the seasons take their course
and etch their stubborn markings on our skin;
the fountains of our youth exhaust their source.
The end, though not yet near, knows to begin.

Wine doesn't taste the same—a stronger brew
is needed to affect a certain glow.
Old jokes are funny—harder with the new.
Our bodies fighting age, but blow by blow,
they're losing—hope to last till later rounds,
but in the meantime, put up a good fight.
Oh, not as dire as that, don't make those sounds!
The day, it may be over, but the night
is plush, dark velvet, and the hunter's moon
is glorious, so let's not leave too soon.

LOVE SONNETS

A sonnet need not always be for love,
but yet it's love, and in its purest form.

It need not venerate the Lord Above;
an English student, sitting in her dorm,
arranging phrases this way, that way, till
a sentence sounds just right: it draws, it sings!
A river rushing forward, never still.
Stars shoot across the sky, pluck cosmic strings.

Is it a sonnet if no lover hears
adoring, wooing quatrains of clichés;
a mistress is not moved to happy tears?
The reader must decide. The rulebook says:
Review the guidelines, but let poems rule.

This sonnet written by a loving fool.

NIGHT AND DAY

Day springs, an omelet, sunny side is up.
Night falls, depleted, hash of all that's been.
Day dresses for success, drinks coffee cup.
Night crawls to bed. She's naked and obscene.

Reflections of each other, they attempt
to meet whenever Time itself allows,
and treasure those brief moments that exempt,
allowing Night to waken, Day to drowse.

Can poetry exist, and have its say
without the daily rhythm of our lives?
On tide-locked planets, absent night or day,
do sonnets praise both mistresses and wives?

I do not know, but I do hope to read
their poetry. It's alien indeed.

TO MY FATHER

A Hallmark holiday, as if one needs
a staunch reminder of the role he played.
He is long gone, but memories, like weeds,
invade the well-kempt garden that I've made
of my adulthood. Where would I be now,
if not for words read to me as a child?
Would freedom mean as much without the how?
I grew up free. Free of the loathed, reviled
regime that stole his youth, a Gulag camp.
How can one thank for every sunny day,
for a blue passport with a precious stamp,
a title that reads, simply, U.S.A.
For children that grew up without a fear.
A happy day for me. I shed a tear.

Places, Everybody

ON BOURBON STREET

The drums fall silent as the rock guitar
cries mournfully; the vodka burns my throat.
The saxophone joins in, and as they spar
I draw another twenty from my coat.

The table to the right is short on beer;
the waitress makes her rounds, a loaded tray.
Exhausted, but her smile appears sincere.
I wave, the bill in hand as if to pay.

"Another one?" she asks, points at the drink.
The Bloody Mary about halfway done—
"You busy later?"—a half-hearted wink.
"Fuck you," she mouths, then pats my hand, and gone.

The cocktails drown in atmosphere and beat.
The poet and his muse, on Bourbon Street.

DEAR FLORENCE

Your galleries are groaning with the strain
of masterpieces chomping at the bit.
Each seeks to earn its eminent domain,
"Pick me, pick me," they shout into the street.

Here, Donatello's David tips his hat
acknowledging his famous counterpart,
and Venus on the shell, yeah, she's all that,
her ministry's affairs are of the heart.

Lorenzo the Magnificent stands tall,
these cobblestones were once beneath his feet.
Savonarola's faithful on a roll,
plain politics the cause of their defeat

Enlightenment, it's here you found your home.

My admiration,

and Yours Truly,

Rome

JERUSALEM

Jerusalem, I'll be your violin,
a mournful Kaddish speaking for the dead.
For those among the grieving, we begin
by praising the almighty in their stead.

Your golden city gates long since torn down,
and Golgotha still groans under the weight
of suffering by those who wore your crown
and lost their heavy heads as was their fate.

And yet I sing for you, Jerusalem,
the triumph of my people, and their doom.
What does HaShem require: just one lamb?
Or must we slaughter hope, still in the womb?

I'll sing your song, both this year, and the next,
and be your violin—you know the text.

BRYCE

The sculptor that first chiseled Bryce's peaks,
with godly hammer and divine techniques,
was it for bobcats and for Steller's jays?
Is that the audience that sculptor seeks?

I drink the landscape in, still in a daze.
The jealous sun looks out and sends its rays;
lights up the powdered rocks, a candy land,
flambé dessert, the mountains are ablaze.

Could he have known, the sculptor, had he planned,
the color, composition of the sand,
so that when man first came upon these hills
he'd stop and stare, attempt to understand?

Just chance, you'll say, the working of free wills,
but there's the desert, and the sculpture thrills.

OCEAN VIEWS

Waves crash, exhausted, foaming at the mouth,
and turn my footprints into shallow graves.
So angry, the Atlantic—further south,
the beach may plain give up—for now, behaves,

but angry, and the churning sand can tell.
The hermit crabs, they too make their regrets,
and hasten to avoid each coming swell.
Escape, that's if the surging ocean lets.

A lonely seagull grabs a plastic cup.
Triumphant, it will launch into the fray,
so confident it's had enough to sup.
The salty water helps it down its prey.

My walk is over. Waves regain their blues.
Across the street, new condos—ocean views.

LESS TRAVELED

He wondered, as the road unraveled:
How do you pick the one less traveled?
The footprints on the beaten path,
seductive with their simple math,
offer the glimpse of a solution,
and so he reached a resolution,
and turned to where no foot had stepped.
No creature stumbled, wagon crept.
A highway flawless and pristine.
Ready to see those sights, unseen,
that mark the difference of a life,
but all he saw was the same strife.
The road less traveled, it turns out
ends the same way, ends in a route.

EASTER ISLAND

As pent-up passions knot the very air
and waters churn, a maelstrom in the void,
the shore gives way. Unanswered goes the prayer
and statues, stern, that men stood up, devoid

of any power to arrest or stop

the ocean, resolute though they may be,

are soon submerged. They failed to either slow

or much less halt the advent of the sea.
What's left then, to the sculptors of the stone?
More statues, bigger ones, or better gods?
The old ones are still clinging to their throne.
Who'll win, the sculptors or the gods? What odds
would you assign here? Come, and place a bet,

but do not call it. Please. At least not yet.

ALWAYS HAVE PARIS

Well, let's talk Paris if you think we must.
Our moonwalks up and down Champs-Élysées.
Was any of it more than wanton lust,
a textbook love affair, a sad cliché?
The promises, the lies, oh, but we knew!
We knew, but let the city have its way,
and so, the days we had, too few, too few,
would not allow for truth. We had to say:
"I love you," "I will leave her," "I'll come back."
"I'll always," "I'll remember," "I'll be free."
Our hearts, as if they've always had the knack,
pretended not to hear and not to see.
Alone now, in the early winter chill . . .
And Paris? Never had it, never will.

SONNET STATION

Announcer says: Approaching Sonnet Station.
My ears perk up. I'm going to Nantucket.
The book is stillborn, midway through gestation.
Nantucket being where one goes when fuck it.

I chuckle at the thought of all the has-beens'
debating whether dots must have two spaces.
The dusty bookstores and their empty dust bins;
the never-will-bes in their coffee places.

What kind of town would call itself a "sonnet"?
A poet colony? Is it contagious?
Romantics seize your soul and feast upon it,
and rhyme-a-dozens masquerade as sages?

Full stop. Doors open. Sky is grey with rain.
I hesitate . . . then leave doubt on the train.

Commentary

FREEDOM'S PRICE

What's freedom's price? Must life be offered up,
defending ancient scribbles on a page?
Must blood be drawn, a sacrificial cup,
and tyrants met head on, with righteous rage?

Our common and inalienable rights,
secured through endless toil and sacrifice,
sit squarely in the tyrant's bloody sights.
We're summoned once again to name their price.

The ends must always struggle with their means
or fear becoming that which they abhor.
Death is the easy choice. Well-oiled machines
rush to seduce with promises of war.

Search for the answer, but let freedom ring.
Let no man be a slave and let no man be king.

EXISTENTIAL QUESTIONS

Philosophers and princes have the time
to ponder on the vagaries of life.
The rest of us deal daily with the climb
or worse, avoiding pestilence and strife.

The privilege of it, you've but to ask
the famous question—not an online poll.
Outrageous fortune relishes the task.
The rest of us sling arrows, rant, and troll.

To be or not to be—no shopping list.
No tradeoff between gasoline and milk,
nor a defense against a bloodied fist.
The rest of us must manage with their ilk.

And existential questions? Like I said,
they're best when served with fragrant wine and bread.

TYRANT

When reason is on trial and justice bends
until it is the opposite of truth,
and means adjust according to their ends,
and theater succeeds the voting booth—
What lies beneath the plastic of your smile,
your practiced adlibs and impromptu rants?
Too generous to call your nature guile;
too dangerous to think adoring chants
are not just what they are. Your acolytes
are eager to accept whatever comes,
as rhetoric descends from lower heights
and rhythmic thumping beats words into drums.
May terror fill your every waking moment,

and sleep desert your bed. There's no atonement.

BANALITY OF EVIL

Banality of evil—what a phrase!
Exasperated, we must not abide
as decency itself is set ablaze,
and pragmatism dictates we set aside
the values that were taught to us from birth.
The horrors, reminiscent of a reel
in black and white, charred edges, burning Earth.
Banality, is that how you must feel,
when watching Death's macabre and gruesome smile?
Eye sockets full of flies, drained of all light;
banality? Let's ponder this awhile . . .
Give right a bit more time to challenge might?
Never again, we say—just one more time.
The worth of a cliché is but a dime.

METROPOLIS

Forgotten temples dot the cityscape
where humans used to sacrifice their lives.
The avenues that offered no escape;
their spirit lives, but nothing else survives.
The wind howls as no canine ever did.
The rats and roaches long since disappeared.
Dust devils dance dark alleys that once hid
the seedy city's waste, and those that feared
the cleansing light of day. No need to hide,
the sunlight barely permeates the clouds.
The sidewalks, emptied long ago, abide,
but wait in vain to host returning crowds.
Where's everyone? What happened here? You know.
And this? Merely my long "I told you so."

Seasonal

THE ARGUMENT

This happened once: the seasons disagreed.
Which one of them was truly made for love?
Unable to resolve it, they proceed
to seek advice from Zeus, who reigns above.

Old Winter said: It's clear, I am the one.
Wine by the fireplace, can that be beat?
And Autumn said: When trees, touched by the sun,
show off their colors, lovers feel complete.

And Summer was so confident, she said:
When coats come off and water makes its splash,
and warmer nights invite you to their bed.
Why even argue, no need to rehash . . .

And Spring? A no-show, though she would be missed.
Grabbed by her lover, stayed behind, and kissed . . .

SPRING SERENADE

The forest, soon to wake up, makes a sound
of stretching sleepy limbs from head to toe.
The snowdrops peek above the thawing ground,
and squirrels settle scores with friend and foe.
A songbird dares to test its vocal chords;
the orchestra then joins the exercise.
A symphony presented for awards,
ambition as important as pure size.
How do they know, the critters low and high,
that time has come to sing their way to love?
That serenade they must, however shy?
Was there a signal sent from up above?
All that exists must celebrate the spring,
and so I join the chorus, and I sing.

SAILS OF SUMMER

the wave tops chase each other to the beach
and crash, exhausted, foaming at the mouth.
I sit, observing, safely out of reach,
admiring sailboats leaving for the South.

the water's ageless color wets the sand,
erasing childish forts and fragile hearts.
the hermit crabs don't dare to make a stand
and move their pearly homes to finer parts.

the moon will soon give up its vain attempt
to purify the spot on which I sit.
the waves break in frustration and contempt,
their froth recedes as they admit defeat.

the last sail leans to starboard and winks out.
they're gone now, till the summer makes them sprout

WITCH'S HOUSE

As Marvel superheroes roam the lands
in search of carbohydrates stashed about,
and candies, seized by little, greedy hands,
exhaust supplies, an existential route,
I wonder, is it Hallmark? They're to blame
for this extinction of my M&Ms?
Is there no limit, no proverbial shame?
Their parents, from the Ganges to the Thames,
do they no longer teach the little tikes?
Take some—and leave some for the next to come.
Have you seen candy prices? I mean, yikes!
You'd think it grows on trees—it does for some.
Oh well, I sigh, replenishing the bag
Don't mind me now, I'm just a tired old hag.

AUTUMN

"Dear Autumn," Summer said, "please choose a name
that's shorter and much easier to spell."
And Winter added, echoing the same:
"Indeed, please do, and simpler in the tell."

"I like my name," said Autumn, but the Spring
chimed in with her characteristic charm:
(the rumor has it, they've had quite a fling)
"C'mon, dear Autumn, truly, what's the harm?"

So Autumn, thus persuaded, worked to choose
a name that would be pleasing to the ear,
and easier to spell among "who's who"s
and worthy of a poet's doting cheer.

But on occasion, it enjoys just Autumn.
The leaves descend, as always, to the bottom.

YULE

Is there a cure for seasonal malaise?
A healing balm, a cure, a salve, a poultice?
A kindling to light and set ablaze
the endless grey of winter? It's the solstice.
The day starts clawing back what it had lost.
The smells of pine and balsam fill the cottage,
and manmade magic sparkles in the frost,
(to beat the Joneses, do not spare the wattage).
St. Nicholas, as always, checks it twice—
He'd best complete his shopping for the naughty.
(more likely it is really for the nice,
the parents of the naughty are too snotty)
A few more days, and then the New Year beckons.
Count down from ten: you have a few more seconds.

A Few Final Notes

PAGANINI

The bow: a scepter, nay, a wizard's wand.
Each minor note a key into your heart.
Devoid of an accompanying grand,
the strumming violin plays every part.

Concerto for your soul; soon, heaven's gates
swing open, and the angel, hands on chin,
is seemingly oblivious as fates,
both innocent and guilty as all sin,

stream into paradise. Hosannas pause,
the host stunned into silence . . . notes play on.
A figure, shadowy, appears. His paws
still smoldering; the evening has been won.

"You miss me yet?" A question, and a vow.
No hint of modesty, he takes a bow.

CSÁRDÁS MONTI

The virtuoso's eyes are firmly closed,
no need to see the notes he knows by heart.
The bow takes flight, raw fingers, unopposed,
life of their own, each chooses where to dart,
as Csárdás, oh sweet Csárdás fills the air,
and picks up pace, smiles break out in the stands.
And as you follow, the composer's flare
astonishes, how do the metal strands
not set the bow on fire? How can man
even come close to Monti's breakneck pace,
and do it with such joy, how can his plan
defined in these majestic notes that race
each other in a frantic, splendid dance,
how can it be? Just listen. Here's your chance . . .

MOONLIGHT SONATA

The moonlight oozes from the stately grand
as birdlike fingers stroke the checkered keys.
Time seemingly forgets its second hand,
a drop of golden amber set to freeze.
C-Minor echoes through the concert hall,
draped in a velvet burgundy on oak.
The chandelier's on dim as shadows shawl
the audience in leisurely baroque.
The tempo's picking up, a stately dance.
Wrists up and down, a peacock's mannered gait,
and then, excited, clasping at their chance,
they race across the keyboard to their fate.
Could but a poem match that final note,
the poet, could say, quitting: "all she wrote."

ABOUT A. GEE

GEE has been playing with words since he was little, but has only recently been persuaded to share. Fluent in multiple languages, his initial forays into poetry were in translating Pushkin for his children while staying true to meter and form.

The dark early days of Covid reignited his writing itch. He self-published his first poetry collection, My*th Takes: Rhyme and Reason in the Age of Entitlement*, before focusing almost solely on the sonnet form, which resulted in *Sonnet Station*. His new projects include a second sonnet collection, *a translation of Pushkin's Ruslan and Ludmilla, a*nd a historical fantasy novel*, A King's Lot.*

Originally from the Transnistria region of Moldova and the former Soviet Union, he now splits his time between New Jersey and Texas, where he resides with his wife, children, and six grandchildren.

ABOUT THE PRESS

Unsolicited Press is based out of Portland, Oregon and focuses on the works of the unsung and underrepresented. As a womxn-owned, all-volunteer small publisher that doesn't worry about profits as much as championing exceptional literature, we have the privilege of partnering with authors skirting the fringes of the lit world. We've worked with emerging and award-winning authors such as Amy Shimshon-Santo, Brook Bhagat, Elisa Carlsen, Tara Stillions Whitehead, and Anne Leigh Parrish.

Learn more at unsolicitedpress.com. Find us on Instagram, X, Facebook, Pinterest, Bsky, Threads, YouTube, and LinkedIn. Unsolicited Press also writes a snarky newsletter on Substack.

www.ingramcontent.com/pod-product-compliance
Lightning Source LLC
LaVergne TN
LVHW092056060526
838201LV00047B/1417